FRED FLINTSTONE'S ADVENTURES with WEDGES

Just Split!

by Mark Weakland

illustrated by Christian Cornia

CAPSTONE PRESS
a capstone imprint

Plastic and rubber doorstops
are used to keep doors open.

Wheel chocks are wedges.
They keep wheels from rolling.

When combined with wheels and axles, wedges can help us do a lot of hard work.

These logs need splitting! In this log splitter, the wood is the load. A strong force drives a wedge into the wood. The short, thick wedge moves the load by separating the wood. That's how work gets done, right, Barney?

A wedge plays an important part in a log splitter.

Right, Fred!

Like a nail, a railroad spike is a strong wedge. It anchors the track to the tie.

The sharp edge of a chisel is a useful wedge. More force is created when you hit the chisel with a hammer.

Wedges are simple machines that make our lives better. They help us do all kinds of work. Wedges hold things in place and hold things together. They also lift and separate. Every time I sit down after a long day, I give thanks for wedges. **Yabba-dabba-doo!**

Glossary

chisel—a tool with a flat, sharp end used to cut stone or wood

chock—a wedge or block placed against an object to hold it steady

fiber—a long, thin thread of material, such as cotton, wool, or silk

force—a push or pull exerted upon an object

gravity—a force that pulls objects together

inclined plane—a slanting surface that is used to move objects to different levels

lever—a bar that turns on a resting point and is used to lift items

load—an object that moves when a force is applied

separate—to set apart

Read More

LaMachia, Dawn. *Wedges at Work.* Zoom in on Simple Machines. New York: Enslow Publishing, 2016.

Oxlade, Chris. *Making Machines with Ramps and Wedges.* Simple Machine Projects. Chicago: Capstone Raintree, 2015.

Roza, Greg. *Wedges.* Simple Machine Science. New York: Gareth Stevens Publishing, 2013.

Internet Sites

FactHound offers a safe, fun way to find Internet sites related to this book. All of the sites on FactHound have been researched by our staff.

Here's all you do:

Visit *www.facthound.com*

Type in this code: 9781491484777

Super-cool stuff! Check out projects, games and lots more at
www.capstonekids.com

Index

Look for all the books in the series:

Thanks to our adviser for his expertise, research, and advice:
Paul Ohmann, PhD, Associate Professor of Physics
University of St. Thomas, St. Paul, Minnesota

Published in 2016 by Capstone Press, A Capstone Imprint
1710 Roe Crest Drive, North Mankato, Minnesota 56003
www.mycapstone.com

Library of Congress Cataloging-in-Publication Data
Weakland, Mark, author.
  Fred Flintstone's adventures with wedges : just split! / by
Mark Weakland ; illustrated by Christian Cornia.
  pages cm — (Flintstones explain simple machines
Summary: "Popular cartoon character Fred Flintstone
explains how wedges work and how he uses simple
machines in his daily life"—Provided by publisher.
Audience: 6–8.
Audience: K to grade 3.
ISBN 978-1-4914-8477-7 (library binding)
ISBN 978-1-4914-8483-8 (eBook PDF)
1. Wedges—Juvenile literature. 2. Simple machines—
Juvenile literature. I. Cornia, Christian, 1975- illustrator. II.
Title. III. Title: Adventures with wedges. IV. Series: Weakland,
Mark. Flintstones explain simple machines.
TJ1201.W44W43 2016
621.8—dc23   2015024736

Editorial Credits
Editor: Alesha Halvorson
Designer: Ashlee Suker
Creative Director: Nathan Gassman
Media Researcher: Tracy Cummins
Production Specialist: Kathy McColley

The illustrations in this book were created digitally.

Image Credits
iStockphoto: adam bennie, 7; Shutterstock: haak78, 9, Iryna
Rasko, 15, Louella938, 5, Tyler Olson, 13, Gene Krebs, 11

Printed in the United States of America in
North Mankato, MN. 092015 009221CGS16